7 Keys to Maximizing Your Potential
and Enjoying Everyday Life

YOUR BEST LIFE
EVER!

PEDRO OKORO

No matter your current circumstances,
your best life is still out in front of you.

#DareToBelieve

YOUR BEST LIFE
EVER!

For Olatundé
You're one in a million!

"*Impossible is just a big word thrown around by small men who find it easier to live in the world they've been given than to explore the power they have to change it. Impossible is not a fact. It's an opinion. Impossible is not a declaration. It's a dare. Impossible is potential. Impossible is temporary. Impossible is nothing.*"

—Adidas ad, *ESPN: The Magazine*

ENDORSEMENTS

"Brilliant, engaging and an inspirational masterpiece!"
—Dr. T. Ayodele Ajayi
Author, *Footprints of Giants*. London, United Kingdom

"How many of us are still waiting to live our Best Life Ever because we have convinced ourselves it's not for us? Where there was once a dream, there are now excuses . . . Exploding in this book is the truth about the meaning of the word impossible. *A word that seems to be just an ordinary, everyday word in our vocabularies, but which in truth has an amazing power over our lives. Pastor Pedro brilliantly unfolds for us, step by step, the mistakes we make as we fall for the trap the enemy sets out for us in order to keep us from ever living our Best Life Ever. In the pages of this book, we find seven golden nuggets of wisdom that will lead us toward breaking free from the lies that have aborted our dreams!"*
—Elsie J. Ruiz
Founder, Shepherd's Way International, Inc.,
Cumming, GA, USA

"Very exciting and faith building!"
—Pastor Ash Kotecha
Milton Keynes, United Kingdom

"Where we are met with cynicism and doubt and fear and those who tell us that we can't, we will respond with that timeless creed that sums up the spirit of the American people in three simple words—Yes, we can."

—Barack Obama, Forty-Fourth President of the United States

• • •

"'What do you mean, "If I can"?' Jesus asked. 'Anything is possible if a person believes.'"

— Mark 9:23, New Living Translation

• • •

"Nothing is impossible, the word itself says 'I'm possible'!"

—Audrey Hepburn

• • •

"Impossible is two letters too long."

—American Express Commercial

ALSO BY PEDRO OKORO:

*Crushing the Devil: Your Guide to Spiritual Warfare
and Victory in Christ*

Desmascarando as Artimanhas do Inimigo

*The Ultimate Guide to Spiritual Warfare: Learn to Fight
from Victory, Not for Victory!*

*Vivendo melhor do que nunca: 7 Chaves para maximizar
o seu potencial e aproveitar a sua vida diária*

CONNECT WITH PEDRO

On Facebook: https://www.facebook.com/pedrookoro7

On Twitter: https://twitter.com/Pedrookoro

Via his blog: http://www.pedrookoro.com/

YOUR BEST LIFE EVER!

Published by
Pedro Sajini Publishing
London, United Kingdom
www.pedrookoro.com/publishing

ISBN 13: 9780993303036
ISBN 10: 0993303036

Printed in the United States

Cover design by David Litwin, Pure Fusion Media (www.purefusionmedia.com)

ACKNOWLEDGMENTS

I would like to thank my daughter, Mychaela, for the excellent work she did on the final draft. I love you, Kayla!

As always, my special thanks to my editor, Rachel Starr Thomson, author, performer, writing coach, and my destiny helper. *Rachel, you rock!*

You can connect with Rachel via her website at http://www.rachelstarrthomson.com.

CONTENTS

Break with convention.
Start believing!

THE WORD *IMPOSSIBLE* DIDN'T EXIST IN THE BEGINNING!

"Impossible is just a big word thrown around by small men who find it easier to live in the world they've been given than to explore the power they have to change it."

—Adidas

"Truly I tell you, if you have faith as small as a mustard seed, you can say to this mountain, 'Move from here to there,' and it will move. Nothing will be impossible for you."

—Matthew 17:20, New International Version

• • •

Impossible is a relatively modern word, having originated from Old French in the late fourteenth century. The comparatively young age of the word makes me believe it did not exist at creation. Certainly not on God's part, as he spoke the world into existence!

But what does the word *impossible* actually mean? The *Chambers 21st Century Dictionary* defines *impossible* as "not capable of happening, being done,"[1] and *unable* as "not able; not

> *The word* impossible *did not exist at creation!*

having sufficient strength, skill, or authority to do something."[2] According to the *Oxford Dictionary of English, impossible* means "not able to occur, exist, or be done."[3] The *Chambers 21st Century Dictionary* then defines *possible* as "achievable; able to be done, capable of happening; imaginable; conceivable."[4]

The word *impossible* as used in the New Testament is from the Greek word *adunate* (pronounced *ad-oo-nat-eh-o*) and means "to be unable."[5] So essentially, in every language, *impossible* means *cannot be done.*

Scripture makes it very clear that *with God,* nothing shall be impossible, and there's nothing too hard or too difficult for God.

> *"Is anything too hard for the LORD?"*
>
> —Genesis 18:14, NIV

So how did the word *impossible* become a part of our vocabulary?

This is what I think happened (and this is me just letting my imagination run free): a long time ago, certain people who could neither fulfill their purpose in life nor realize their full potential found that they needed an explanation or justification for their failure and ineptitude. They came up with the word *impossible,* a big word that in reality denotes nothing.

Impossible is just an excuse!

Impossible is just an excuse!

For many of us, the word *impossible* not only robs us of our future but even of our enjoyment of present-day life. We feel stuck and frustrated. When we walk in faith, we are given the key to joy in everyday life as well, able to live life fully and freely.

To maximize your potential, you must delete the word impossible from your thinking!

To maximize your potential and be everything God created you to be, you must delete the word *impossible* from your thinking and worldview. But how do you remove this word from your language? How do you unlock the treasure trove of possibility that's tucked away within you, thereby maximizing your potential? What does it take to walk on water in your everyday life? How do you live a life where *impossible* is nothing? And how do you enjoy everyday life?

To answer these questions, let's take a look at the story of a man who sought help for his epileptic son. The story is found in the New Testament. We are not told this man's name, so I have decided to call him Matt Abrahamson.

However, before we talk about Matt, let me quickly point out that there are at least four major occasions where we find the words *possible* and *impossible* and their variants *too difficult* and *too hard* in the Bible. In three of them, we are taught that nothing is impossible, too difficult, or too hard for God. That's fair enough, as God is all-powerful!

Here are the first three occasions:

- In Genesis 18:13–14, the Lord asks Abraham, "Is anything too hard for the Lord?"
- In Jeremiah 32:17 and 27, God and Jeremiah are having a conversation. The Lord says, "I am the Lord, the God of all mankind. Is anything too hard for me?" Jeremiah then responds, "Ah, Sovereign Lord, you have made the heavens and the earth by your great power and outstretched arm. Nothing is too hard for you."
- In Luke 1:34–37, we see Mary in a conversation with the archangel Gabriel. It ends with Gabriel assuring Mary, "For with God nothing shall be impossible."

However, the fourth time the word is used, Jesus places a distinctly different take on it. Unlike the other occasions, where the emphasis is on the omnipotence of God, here Jesus introduces the concept that nothing will be impossible for *you*. Jesus is not saying nothing will be impossible for God, but that *nothing will be impossible for you!*

Now, if you're ready, let's read the story of Matt Abrahamson, as told brilliantly by Eugene H. Peterson in *The Message* translation of the Bible:

At the bottom of the mountain, they were met by a crowd of waiting people. As they approached, a man came out of the crowd and fell to his knees begging, "Master, have mercy on my son. He goes out of his mind and suffers terribly, falling into seizures. Frequently he is pitched into the fire, other times into the river. I brought him to your disciples, but they could do nothing for him."

Jesus said, "What a generation! No sense of God! No focus to your lives! How many times do I have to go over these things? How much longer do I have to put up with this? Bring the boy here." He ordered the afflicting demon out—and it was out, gone. From that moment on the boy was well. When the disciples had Jesus off to themselves, they asked, "Why couldn't we throw it out?"

"Because you're not yet taking God seriously," said Jesus. "The simple truth is that if you had a mere kernel of faith, a poppy seed, say, you would tell this mountain, 'Move!' and it would move. There is nothing you wouldn't be able to tackle."

As they were regrouping in Galilee, Jesus told them, "The Son of Man is about to be betrayed to some people who want nothing to do with God. They will murder him—and three days later he will be raised alive." The disciples felt terrible. When they arrived at Capernaum, the tax men came to Peter and asked, "Does your teacher pay taxes?"

Peter said, "Of course." But as soon as they were in the house, Jesus confronted him. "Simon, what do you think? When a king levies taxes, who pays—his children or his subjects?" He answered, "His subjects."

Jesus said, "Then the children get off free, right? But so we don't upset them needlessly, go down to the lake, cast a hook, and pull in the first fish that bites. Open its mouth and you'll find a coin. Take it and give it to the tax men. It will be enough for both of us."[6]

What is the essence and relevance of this story? What is the Lord teaching us here? How does this passage of Scripture answer the questions posed earlier—*How do you unlock and stir up the potential that's locked inside of you? How do you acquire the faith or belief that Jesus was talking about, such that impossible is nothing to you? And how do you enjoy everyday life?*

I will spend this rest of the book answering these questions and unpacking the new concept of possibility introduced by Jesus.

Chapter 1:

CONNECT WITH
THE DIVINE

*"God makes each one of us for the time into which we are born.
He creates us for a purpose. Our job is to know him well,
discover what He created us to do, and then do it for all
we're worth for the rest of our lives."*

—Robin Lee Hatcher, *Fit to Be Tied*

*"Everything got started in him and finds its purpose in him.
He was there before any of it came into existence and holds
it all together right up to this moment."*

—Colossians 1:16–17, *The Message*

• • •

Like many of us today, Matt Abrahamson had problems that he took in stride. But there was one particular problem he found overwhelming. His teenage son, Josh, had epilepsy, caused by problems with his brain not developing properly during childhood.

Josh would often go out of his mind and suffer terribly, often falling into severe seizures. Frequently he was pitched into the fire; other times into the river. Josh's epilepsy was incurable and could only be controlled by medication. The doctors prescribed antiepilepsy drugs (AEDs), which Josh took religiously.

However, Matt wanted more for Josh. He wasn't content with simply managing and controlling the condition. He wanted a cure for his beloved son. When the doctors couldn't help him, he decided to seek help outside of medical science.

A DIVINE ENCOUNTER

Matt's search led him to a divine encounter. He heard about Jesus and learned that his disciples were in the county, and he decided to give him a try. However, not wanting to trouble Jesus, he decided to take Josh to the disciples instead. Unfortunately, they could do nothing for him. Undeterred, Matt decided to see the main man himself, whatever it would take. He waited to see Jesus. And his perseverance paid off.

Matt found Jesus at the foot of a mountain. A crowd of people were surrounding Jesus, but he managed to get in front of him. You could say Matt had a personal relationship with Jesus, because he knew where to find Jesus and how to get his attention. He then knelt before him in worship.

WHY CONNECT WITH JESUS?

There are so many reasons to connect with Jesus. Here are just a couple to reflect upon.

> *Everything got started in Jesus and finds its purpose in him.*

1. Everything got started in him. Jesus began the beginning! Not only that, he holds everything together! Everything got started in Jesus and finds its purpose in him.

> For everything, absolutely everything, above and below, visible and invisible, rank after rank after rank of angels—everything got started in him and finds its purpose in him. He was there

before any of it came into existence and holds it all together right up to this moment.[1]

2. He is the solution to the God-shaped hole.

In the words of Blaise Pascal, "there is a God-shaped vacuum in the heart of every man which cannot be filled by any created thing, but only by God the Creator, made known through Jesus Christ."[2]

Wayne Stiles put it this way:

God hardwired each of us with a void only he can fill. Here's what that means practically:

> *God hardwired each of us with a void only he can fill!*

- If you break free from bondage to alcohol but fill that void with anything but Jesus, another bondage will replace it.
- If you wiggle loose from an emotional dependency on relationships but ignore a relationship with the Lord, another addiction will take its place.
- If you struggle with a meaningless, empty existence, buying another boat, taking another job, or getting another spouse won't fill the void.

Only God fills the chasm. Everything else only deepens it.[3]

KNOWING JESUS AS SAVIOR AND LORD

> *God does not have grandchildren!*

It should come as no surprise, therefore, that the first of our seven keys is *connecting with the Divine.* I am not asking you to become religious. Instead, I am inviting you to consider a personal relationship with Jesus. Do you know Jesus personally for yourself? Are you born again? Your parents may be Christians, but that does not make you a Christian. God does not have grandchildren!

The disciples disappointed Matt because they couldn't heal his son, but he knew where to find the Lord. He knew how to find the Lord. He knew how to approach the Lord.

> I am the Gate. Anyone who goes through me will be cared for—will freely go in and out, and find pasture. A thief is only there to steal and kill and destroy. I came so they can have real and eternal life, more and better life than they ever dreamed of.[4]

Jesus is the author of life. He created it. He holds it together. He came to give you Eternal Life—a better life than you could ever dream of, not only here on earth, but more importantly in the world to come! Your life finds its purpose in him.

> I am trying here to prevent anyone saying the really foolish thing that people often say about Him: I'm ready to accept Jesus as a great moral teacher, but I don't accept his claim to be God. That is the one thing we must not say. A man who was merely a man and said the sort of things Jesus said would not be a great moral teacher. He would either be a lunatic—on the level with the man who says he is a poached egg—or else he would be the Devil of Hell. You must make your choice. Either this man was, and is, the Son of God, or else a madman or something worse. You can shut him up for a fool, you can spit at him and kill him as a demon or you can fall at his feet and call him Lord and God, but let us not come with any patronizing nonsense about his being a great human teacher. He has not left that open to us. He did not intend to. (C.S. Lewis, *Mere Christianity*)

Jesus is the key to enjoying everyday life!

Jesus is the key to enjoying everyday life. If you know Jesus, you know life. On the other hand, if there's no Jesus in your life, then there's no life! If you don't know him as your Savior and

Lord, why not connect with him right now? A simple prayer will do. Tell him you believe he died for your sins. Then invite him into your heart as your Savior and Lord.

If you're already a Christian, then stay connected. Stay connected to God. Stay in faith. Give all your worries and burdens to Jesus, so you can travel light!

> *"You have made us for yourself, O Lord, and our hearts are restless until they rest in you."*
>
> —St. Augustine of Hippo

Chapter 2:

DISCOVER YOUR PURPOSE

"You will never flourish if you attempt something other than what God has called you to do!"

—A.L. Andrews

"We must quickly carry out the tasks assigned us by the one who sent us. The night is coming, and then no one can work."

—John 9:4, New Living Translation

• • •

Matt Abrahamson knew what he wanted to achieve in life. He was single-minded and focused. Ever since his son, Josh, became epileptic, Matt's entire world had revolved around getting a cure. That became his purpose, the driving force and the reason for his existence—getting a cure for his son. He lived for the moment when his son would become completely healed.

Regardless of the circumstances of your birth, there is a purpose to your life. You are not an accident. God had you in his plan long before your parents even set eyes on each other. There is a reason for your existence. There's more to your life than just eating, drinking, going to bed, and waking up.

Your purpose is what God created you for!

PURPOSE? WHAT'S THAT?

Your purpose is what God created you for, your God-given assignment. It is your calling. *Purpose* and *calling* are sometimes used interchangeably. Purpose is the answer to the questions "What on earth am I doing here?" and "What do I want to do with my life?" God created you, and only in him can you find your purpose. That's one reason you don't *determine* your purpose. Instead, you *discover* it!

> *Regardless of the circumstances of your birth, there is a purpose to your life!*

In Acts 13:2, the Holy Spirit said, "Set apart for me Barnabas and Saul for the work to which I have called them." There is a purpose to why you are here in this world. And until you're set apart and separated for what you're called to do, you will not be fulfilled.

> It's in Christ that we find out who we are and what we are living for. Long before we first heard of Christ and got our hopes up, he had his eye on us, had designs on us for glorious living, part of the overall purpose he is working out in everything and everyone.[1]

My nephew, Tega, was just like any seven year old. He was playful, mischievous, and full of energy, and he loved football (soccer to our American friends). And being an Okoro, he was handsome, smart, and had a great future ahead of him.

Then he had a fever and died. Just like that. At the tender age of seven! We were devastated. I felt particularly sorry for my dad, who had lost his first son about six years previously, three months before my older brother's fortieth birthday.

Tega died with all the potential he was created with. The ideas, books, poems, songs, even inventions he might have been born with all died with him. He never had a chance to be what God created him to be. He didn't have the opportunity to ask himself,

"What on earth am I doing here?" However, the real tragedy is that people live to be fifty, sixty, seventy, eighty, or even ninety years of age without fulfilling their purpose.

CLUES TO HELP YOU UNDERSTAND YOUR PURPOSE

So have you found your purpose? Here are some clues as to what it might be:

There's a purpose to why you are here in this world!

- Your talent and the things you are passionate about give an inkling of your purpose. Simon Peter and his brother Andrew were talented fishermen. It therefore doesn't come as a surprise that Jesus told them when he first met them that he would make them fishers of men![2]
- Your purpose is connected to what you want your legacy to be! If you had 365 days to live, what would you do? Some people would probably want to put their house in order, but I suspect most would reevaluate their priorities. Would you do anything differently? Take a moment to reflect on what you would want your obituary to say. How would you want to be remembered?
- Your calling will likely feel familiar to you, yet distant, vague, and mysterious. Familiar in the sense that past lessons and experiences (including past failures) have prepared you for it. Vague and mysterious because it's kind of new and different!
- It should complement the things you're passionate about rather than compete against them. You shouldn't have to choose between the things that make you forget to eat and your purpose!
- It will be bigger than you. It must be so big that you need God and a team of people (I call them "destiny helpers") to help you accomplish it. Even Jesus needed a destiny helper

to help him fulfill his purpose of dying on a cross—Simon of Cyrene, who helped him carry the cross to Calvary.[3]

• Sometimes, pain prepares you for purpose! When this happens, you need to learn from the experience and find a way to turn your pain into purpose. Matt Abrahamson turned the pain of his son's epilepsy into *his* purpose.

TALENTS AND EXPERIENCE WILL PREPARE YOU FOR YOUR CALLING

Your personality type, temperament, talents, and life experiences will help to prepare you for your purpose. In the journey of life, no experience is futile, no matter how difficult, painful, or even catastrophic it may seem!

Your talents are not your purpose, but they will prepare you for it. Although Joseph had the gift of dream interpretation and was passionate about it, his purpose was not to interpret dreams. Joseph was born

> *Joseph was born to preserve lives. That was his purpose!*

to preserve lives during seven years of famine and to make room for the Israelites in Egypt.[4] That was his purpose! However, he could not fulfill his purpose without utilizing his talent of dream interpretation.

Your pain will likewise prepare you for your purpose. Before Joseph could prepare a place for Israel in Egypt, he had to be in Egypt himself, so he was sold into slavery. Secondly, he needed to interpret Pharaoh's dream, so God allowed him to be sent to prison for a crime he did not commit. Why? Well, because he needed to connect with the royal butler who was in the same prison at the time and who would *eventually* recommend him to Pharaoh when he needed somebody to interpret his dream. Interpreting Pharaoh's dream paved the way for Joseph to become prime minister, ultimately helping to fulfill his purpose.

STILL NOT SURE?

If you're still not sure of your calling, why not pray? Ask God to reveal your purpose. Seek God in prayer. He will answer!

> Ask, and it will be given to you; seek, and you will find; knock, and it will be opened to you. For everyone who asks receives, and he who seeks finds, and to him who knocks it will be opened.[5]

To discover and fulfill your purpose, you need vision, which we will consider in the next chapter.

Chapter 3:

LET VISION GUIDE YOU

"The journey toward destiny always begins with VISION.
Vision is the roadmap to your destiny, the picture of your
purpose. Without it, you may find yourself off course—
or worse, going nowhere."

—John Maxwell

"Where there is no vision, the people are unrestrained."
—Proverbs 29:18, New American Standard Bible

• • •

Matt Abrahamson had a vision of his son Josh healed of his epilepsy and living a normal, healthy life free of seizures and medical emergencies. Yes, Josh was epileptic. Yes, he suffered severely. Yes, he often fell into water. And yes, he often fell into fire. However, Matt's vision was of his son totally cured and completely free.

That is why Matt was disappointed when Jesus's disciples could not help him. He knew Jesus could do something. He didn't believe in *impossible!* If in Matt's mind his son had been an incurable epileptic, he wouldn't have bothered to take the problem to Jesus.

WHAT IS VISION?

Vision is a revelation of how to get to your destination in life. It is the GPS or satellite navigation system leading to purpose. Your vision is the answer to the following questions: "How do I achieve my goals?" "How do I fulfill my purpose?" "How do I fulfill my calling?"

Vision is the GPS leading to purpose!

Vision is the ability or faculty of perceiving the future with the mind. It is a divine impression of one's destination that is vividly conjured up in the imagination.

WHY DO YOU NEED VISION?

With vision comes discipline. Vision generates self-control and restraint. On the other hand, without a vision there is neither focus nor self-control. Jesus was able to endure the pain and the agony of the cross because he had a revelation of the joy and glory that were set before him.[1]

Joseph gladly suffered the pain of the pit, eagerly said no to Potiphar's beautiful wife, willingly tolerated the pang of the prison, and readily endured the devastation of the dungeon for the simple reason that he had a mental picture of himself in the palace. He could see in his mind's eye the sun, the moon, and the eleven stars bowing down to him.[2]

HOW DO YOU GET VISION?

Your vision is most likely to be related or connected to what you're most passionate about.

John Maxwell says:

Take some time to LOOK . . .
Within you: What is your passion?

Behind you: How have past lessons and experiences prepared
  you to pursue your passion?
Around you: What's happening to others in this area (the trends)?
Ahead of you: What do you want to accomplish?
Above you: What part does God play in your life and dream?
Beside you: What resources are available to you?
Alongside you: Who can partner with you in this pursuit?[3]

WHAT SHOULD YOU DO WITH VISION?

Write it down. The first thing to do with vision is to write it down.
It's important to write down your vision because it is *usually* for a
future time. Visions are futuristic in nature. *Vision* describes something that is yet to happen but which will eventually be fulfilled.

The prophet Habakkuk wrote:

And the Lord answered me, and said, write the vision, and make
[it] plain upon tables, that he may run that readeth it.[4]

Writing down a vision serves at least two purposes. One, it ensures
you won't forget it, and two, it helps others to understand it, especially if the vision is to be acted upon in your absence.

Communicate it. A good visionary is able to communicate his
vision to others. According to Maxwell, "Good leaders must communicate vision clearly, creatively, and continually."

Be patient. If the fulfillment of the vision seems slow in coming,
wait patiently, because it will surely take place (provided, of course,
that it's in line with your purpose). It will not be unduly delayed.

Act on the vision! According to Joel A. Barker, "Vision without
action is merely a dream. Action without vision just passes the
time. Vision with action can change the world." A Japanese prov-
erb says, "Vision without action is a daydream. Action without
vision is a nightmare."

One of the greatest visionaries of modern times, who is described
as "a pioneer and innovator and the possessor of one of the most

fertile imaginations the world has ever known,"[5] Walt Disney documented his vision of a Disney World of entertainment, complete with an artist's impression of Disney World. And so, although he died before the vision could be fully realized, his older brother and business partner, Roy Disney, was able to return from retirement and execute Walt's vision with the opening of Walt Disney World on October 1, 1971, more than five years after Walt Disney passed away. Today, Walt Disney World Resort in Orlando, Florida, is the number-one tourist attraction in the world.

Matt probably wrote down his vision of Josh living a life free of epilepsy. He would have communicated his vision to his family and to Josh, who went along with him to Jesus. He was patient and didn't give up, even when Jesus's disciples couldn't help him. But most important of all, he acted on his vision. He went looking for Jesus. And that made him fulfill his purpose—he found a cure for Josh!

Chapter 4:

MAXIMIZE YOUR POTENTIAL

"Our graveyards are filled with potential that remained potential. What a tragedy!"

—Dr. Myles Munroe

"God created human beings; he created them godlike, reflecting God's nature. He created them male and female. God blessed them: 'Prosper! Reproduce! Fill Earth! Take charge! Be responsible for fish in the sea and birds in the air, for every living thing that moves on the face of Earth.'"

—Genesis 1:27–28, *The Message*

• • •

God made you in his image. He blessed you and commissioned you to take care of the earth. Not only that, he empowered you to reign and exercise dominion over the rest of creation. He loaded you with all the qualities you could ever need to fulfill your purpose. This has been true for all of us since creation. Although some of those attributes were distorted when Adam and Eve fell in the Garden

There's a phenomenal amount of potential buried deep within you waiting to be extracted!

of Eden, we still retain a phenomenal amount of potential, buried deep within us, waiting to be extracted and put to use.

The only limitation on your life is the one you set yourself!

DON'T LIMIT YOURSELF

The only limitation on your life is the one you set yourself. The potential is there. Everyone has it. The most powerful computer can't even compare with a tiny portion of the human brain. In general, as humans, we use only a fraction of our mental capacity. You are loaded with incredible and limitless potential. You are a masterpiece.

Scott Flansburg, born 1963, is often called a human calculator. Flansburg has been teaching math and entertaining people with his astonishing math skills for more than 20 years. Nicknamed, the Human Calculator, he currently holds the Guinness World Record for adding the same number to itself more times in 15 seconds than a person can do using a calculator. This remarkable ability is what earned him the title of "Fastest Human Calculator."[1]

Throughout Scott's travels, he proves his capacity to perform high-speed addition, subtraction, multiplication, square roots, and even cube roots. More important than showing the skills he has acquired, however, he wants to show others that they already have the ability to perform seemingly difficult math problems without a calculator. He has learned that any student or professional who needs to use math in his or her daily life is only hindered by the calculator. Using Scott's nontraditional tactics, their brains could perform much better.

The word impossible *should be alien to you!*

Considering what is deposited within you, the word *impossible* should be alien to you. Nothing should be impossible for you. I mean absolutely nothing! You have the power of life and death in your tongue. There is no height you cannot scale if you really want to. There is no river you cannot cross if you have the right desire. There is no obstacle you cannot surmount as long as you set your heart to it. No dream is too great.

If you're a Christian, this gets even better, because you have all the resources of heaven at your disposal. You have the greatest force in the universe on the inside. God is with you. God is in you! And you can depend on Jesus, who strengthens, enables, and empowers you through the Holy Spirit. Jesus put it this way: "What do you mean, 'If I can'? Anything is possible if a person believes."[2]

THE MAN WHO SEES WITH HIS FINGERS

Esref Armagan (born 1953) is a man who is maximizing his potential despite great odds. A contemporary Turkish painter, he has been completely blind since birth. He grew up poor and uneducated and never had an art lesson, yet he paints detailed pictures in bright colors and three-point perspective without assistance.

For decades, Armagan was the subject of curiosity, awe, and skepticism in his native Turkey. Then in 2004, he became the subject of scientific brain studies in the United States. The astonishing results have been published in science journals, magazines, and newspapers around the globe.

In 2008 the Discovery Channel aired a documentary that featured Armagan and three others with extraordinary abilities, called *The Real Superhumans*.

In 2009, the automobile giant Volvo commissioned Esref to paint their new model S60 as part of a social media campaign. That painting was auctioned on eBay and sold for $3050, which went to the Canadian nonprofit charity World Blind Union (WBU).

STIR UP YOUR LATENT POTENTIAL

Scott Flansburg and Esref Armagan are not alone. How do you unlock and stir up the latent potential that's locked away inside of you?

1. Dare to dream!

> *"A dream is an inspiring picture of the future that energizes your mind, will, and emotions, empowering you to do everything you can to achieve it."*
>
> —John C. Maxwell

A dream is the starting point to realizing your potential. And while you're at it, dream big! Project into the future. Start dreaming bigger, thinking bigger, praying bigger and expecting bigger! Make a Dream List. God wants to take you where you've never been.

> *"If you can dream it, you can do it."*
>
> —Walt Disney

> *"If you want to reach a goal, you must 'see the reaching' in your own mind before you actually arrive at your goal."*
>
> —Zig Ziglar

> *"All our dreams can come true, if we have the courage to pursue them."*
>
> —Walt Disney

2. Be purpose-driven.

As stated in chapter 2, your purpose is the answer to the questions "Why am I here?" and "What on earth am I doing here?" You don't determine your purpose; you discover and find it. You were created by God, and only in him can you find your purpose.

> *"Everything got started in him and finds its purpose in him."*
>
> —Colossians 1:16–17 (MSG)

Jesus was completely purpose-driven. Even his name had something to do with his purpose.

> *"She will give birth to a son, and you are to give him the name*
> *Jesus, because he will save his people from their sins."*
>
> —Matthew 1:21.

Not only that, he was consumed by his purpose. In John 4:34 he said, "My food is to do the will of him who sent me and to finish his work."

3. Cultivate a burning desire to succeed.

What is success? That is very much subjective. According to Stephen Covey, author of *The Seven Habits of Highly Effective People,* "If you carefully consider what you want to be said of you in the funeral experience, you will find your definition of success."

You must believe that God wants to take you where you've never been. Break out of that limited mind-set. You have greatness in you. Where you are isn't where you're supposed to stay.

> *Break out of that limited mind-set!*

> *"There is one quality which one must possess to win, and*
> *that is definiteness of purpose, the knowledge of what*
> *one wants, and a burning desire to possess it."*
>
> —Napoleon Hill

4. Set SMART goals and objectives for yourself.

Develop a clear sense of direction. An important step to realizing your potential is to establish a SMART goal around which to organize a plan of action. The goal must be Specific, Measurable, Attainable, Realistic, and Time-bound.

> *"A goal is a dream with a deadline."*
>
> —Napoleon Hill

Make a list of ten goals you would like to achieve in the next twelve months. Of the ten, highlight the one goal that is the most important of all, the game changer—the one goal that can *in fact* make the other nine goals happen.

Now turn that goal into a question, something like: *How do I earn $1 million in the next twelve months?* Now begin to write down twenty ways you can achieve that goal. You will find that the first ten answers are easy. It will get more difficult as you approach number twenty. But don't give up; stay the course. Go all the way to twenty, no matter how difficult it may seem, and you might just stumble on the answer to your *breakthrough!*

5. Be faithful and committed.

To be faithful is to be committed and trustworthy. Be fully, completely, and totally committed to God. Be trustworthy in whatever he has committed into your hands, recognizing the fact that someday you will be required to render an account of your stewardship to him.[3]

Be reliable. Be dependable.

6. Get started and give it all you've got!

Just do something! Walt Disney once gave this wonderful advice: "The way to get started is to quit talking and begin doing." Nelson Mandela added this: "It always seems impossible until it's done." Christopher Reeve put it this way: "So many of our dreams at first seem impossible, then they seem improbable, and then, when we summon the will, they soon become inevitable." And finally, Martin Luther King Jr concludes it this way: "If you can't fly then run, if you can't run then walk, if you can't walk then crawl, but whatever you do you have to keep moving forward."

So get started. And do not despise the days of little beginnings.[4] Although you need to dream big, you may need to start small.

Be the best you can be. Commit to excellence. Be excellent in all you do. The Bible says, "Whatever you do, do well. For when you go

Be the best you can be!

to the grave, there will be no work or planning or knowledge or wisdom."[5]

"The difference between try and triumph is just a little umph!"

—Marvin Phillips

"The difference between ordinary and extraordinary is that little extra."

—Jimmy Johnson

6. Determine to die empty.

It was Paul the apostle who said, "I am already being poured out like a drink offering, and the time for my departure is near. I have fought the good fight, I have finished the race, I have kept the faith."[6]

Like Paul, everyone is born full. You're born loaded with ideas, dreams, and visions. Like Paul, God expects you to be "poured out" as you go through life so that you're completely empty when you die.

Make a quality decision today that you will do your utmost to ensure that your dreams, songs, books, paintings, ideas, visions, inventions, plans, purposes, and all other potential locked away within you will not go with you to your grave.

Chapter 5:

DARE TO BELIEVE

"Believe you can, and you're halfway there!"
—Theodore Roosevelt

"I can do everything through Christ, who gives me strength."
—Philippians 4:13, New Living Translation

• • •

Be positive about the great ideas floating around in your head. If you couldn't achieve them, you wouldn't have them in the first place! Dare to believe. And believe you can!

Belief exists at two levels: belief in God and self-belief. Healthy self-belief is a sense of confidence in what God has deposited within you and what he has made you to become. It is your confidence in God's ability in you. It is having the assurance to be able to declare, "I can do everything through Christ who gives me strength."[1]

|| *Believe you can!*

On the other hand, belief in God is the currency that releases your potential and carries your breakthrough. This belief is also called *faith*, which is the instrument that activates and sets loose the answers to your prayers. Jesus once told a woman who had been suffering from chronic bleeding for twelve years, who had spent all her money on doctors to no avail and who had become a social outcast, "Daughter, your faith has made you well. Go in peace! Be cured from your illness."² This lady, through her faith, was able to activate and set in motion the divine solution to her long-term problem.

You can do the same today, even with the tiniest amount of faith. The type of faith needed to birth your breakthrough is similar to light. Light always dispels darkness, no matter how faint the light may be. The size or quantity is irrelevant.

Jesus couldn't be clearer: "Truly I tell you, if you have faith as small as a mustard seed, you can say to this mountain, 'Move from here to there,' and it will move. Nothing will be impossible for you."³

HOW DOES ONE ACQUIRE FAITH?

Faith comes from three sources, which are not only similar but are actually interrelated:

Inspiration. Inspiration is a sudden brilliant or timely idea that drops into your mind seemingly from nowhere. Inspiration comes from God and sometimes through people who are gifted in their fields.

Revelation. Revelation comes from God as you study the Bible. God can cause a verse of Scripture to jump out at you, empowering you to act in faith.

Information. Sometimes, to get from where you are to where you should be all you need is the right information. There's no telling how much confidence the right information can generate.

"YOUR NAME IS BENJAMIN UNDERWOOD. YOU CAN DO ANYTHING."

Let me tell you about Ben Underwood, who acquired his faith from the positive information his mother fed him! Diagnosed with retinal cancer at the age of two, Ben lost both his eyes at the age of three. He overcame his disability and enjoyed his everyday life thanks to his mother, Aquanetta Gordon, a woman of profound faith who believed nothing was impossible for her son despite his blindness.

No matter what, Ben was going to have confidence that "anything you can do, I can do better." It might take a little more work for him than it did for other people, but I knew Ben wasn't going to stop until he achieved something. I refused to accept that Ben would be blind even though he physically had no eyes. I refused to call him "my blind son" or remind Ben that he was blind. No. It was, "Ben, go play. Just watch out for cars. Your name is Benjamin Underwood, and you can do anything!"[4]

Encouraged by his mother, Ben taught himself to perceive and locate objects by making clicking sounds with his tongue and using the echoes as they bounced off his environment to create a visual image in his mind. He went on to master human echolocation—the ability to detect the size, shape, and location of objects through the reflection of sound waves—and became known as "the boy who could see with sound."

Ben began to use this technique at age three and further improved it so that even the surface of the objects did not matter—metal, wood, or another human being, Ben was able to perceive the distance to objects in his environment by how loud or faint the echo was. Ben never used a guide dog or a white cane in his life. By clicking his tongue and "seeing" the sound waves, Ben could ride his bike on a road, shoot baskets, identify objects, and even play video games! After his unique skill made the news, he was featured in several magazines and TV shows.

Unfortunately, Ben's cancer returned in 2007, and this time, treatment was not able to save his life—but not before he'd lit up the world and showed that *impossible* is nothing! Ben died in January 2009, one week before his seventeenth birthday.

ASPIRE FOR HIGHER AND BETTER

Sometimes to get from where you are to where you need to be, you just need to become sick and tired of your current situation and aspire for higher! When you tell yourself "enough is enough" and aspire for higher and better, you unlock your creative self. You release your creativity. You dare to believe. And heaven backs you!

Esau and Jacob were twin sons of Isaac. Jacob, the younger son, stole Esau's birthright and blessing. When he became aware of this, Esau begged their father for a blessing, any blessing. Isaac's response is very insightful. He told him, "You'll live far from Earth's bounty, remote from Heaven's dew. You'll live by your sword, hand-to-mouth, and you'll serve your brother. *But when you can't take it any more you'll break loose and run free*"[5] (my emphasis). In other words, you, Esau, will be subservient to Jacob. However, when you become sick and tired of being subservient to your younger brother and say to yourself "enough is enough," you will break free!

> *When you tell yourself "enough is enough", and aspire for higher and better, you unlock your creative self!*

WHEN ENOUGH IS ENOUGH

Becoming sick and tired in the manner envisaged by Isaac doesn't just lead to anger, disgust, and discontent, but to a genuine and heartfelt desire for change. This releases your creativity and should lead to corresponding action on your part. Why? Because when the need for something becomes essential, you are forced to find ways of achieving it. Not only that, something spiritual and distinctly mysterious happens: God backs you!

I believe this is what happened to Zara cofounder Mr. Amancio Ortega, who is the richest man in Europe and the wealthiest retailer in the world.[6] According to Ms. Covadonga O'Shea, author of a biography of the Zara founder: "One day [he and] his mother went to pick up some groceries. From below the counter, he heard someone tell his mother, 'Senora . . . we can't give you any more credit.'"

Ms. O'Shea, writing her book in 2012, said that to this day Mr. Ortega still felt shame at the family's inability to pay. "When Amancio was telling me this, he was terribly emotional. And he said to me: 'I was deeply hurt and humiliated.'" He vowed never to let his family suffer poverty again.[7]

That comment to his mother was the kick Ortega needed to become the best that he could be. And it didn't happen overnight. No way! Having vowed never to let his family suffer poverty again, he left school and went to work in a shirt shop. In 1963 he started manufacturing textiles through a small family company before cofounding Zara with his ex-wife, Rosalía Mera, in 1975. By the mid-1980s, Ortega had expanded throughout Spain, and he opened his first store in America in 1989. Today he is the second richest person in the world.

NOW STEP OUT

"Start by doing what is necessary, then what is possible,
and suddenly you are doing the impossible."

—Francis of Assisi

You've been inspired to believe. You've become sick and tired of your present situation. You've received the right information, and now your confidence is sky-high. You've acquired faith through revelation. But that can only take you halfway. You need more. To maximize your potential and enjoy everyday life, you need a little bit extra.

Faith may be a noun, but in practice, it's a verb. It is the nature of faith that it cannot survive on its own. Faith is like a seed, which must be planted to unlock its potential. It needs to be accompanied by corresponding action. Faith requires appropriate deeds to become effective.[8]

A long time ago, Abraham sent his personal assistant on a mission to find a bride for his heir, Isaac. The PA knew he couldn't do this on his own. So he prayed. He was confident that God would guide him to the appropriate young woman. He had belief, but he didn't stop there. Hear his testimony: "I being in the way, the Lord led me."[9] He added practical action to his belief. He stepped out. And he got the right result.

> *Winning starts with beginning!*

It was Joe Sabah who said, "You don't have to be great to start, but you have to start to be great." Just get started. Somebody once said that beginning is half done. Winning starts with beginning. And to begin, you must do something *right now*. Don't wait until the conditions are perfect. They may never be! Don't wait until you're ready. You may never be!

You've got faith. You've got belief. You're confident. Now step out . . . in faith!

Chapter 6:

RIDE OUT THE STORM

"You may encounter many defeats, but you must not be defeated. In fact, it may be necessary to encounter the defeats, so you can know who you are, what you can rise from, how you can still come out of it."

—Maya Angelou

"When you're in rough waters, you will not go down. When you're between a rock and a hard place, it won't be a dead end—Because I am God, your personal God, The Holy of Israel, your Savior."

—Isaiah 43:2–3, The Message

• • •

Ride out the storm. Stay the course. Learn to persevere. The storm will pass. Troubles don't last. Your troubles won't kill you!

Some people give up too easily. At the slightest hint of difficulty, they throw in the towel. Not Matt Abrahamson. He persisted. Even though Jesus's disciples couldn't help his son, he persevered. He did not give up, because he wanted more.

Ron Wayne cofounded Apple with Steve Jobs and Steve Wozniak, providing administrative oversight for the new company. He had a

10 percent stake in the company. Wayne wrote the original Apple partnership agreement, drew the first Apple logo, and wrote the Apple 1 Manual. He later sold his shares back for $800. He didn't stay the course for a variety of personal reasons, which seemed reasonable at the time. But as of April 2016, Wayne's 10 percent stake in Apple Inc. was worth about $60 billion. Imagine if he had ridden out the storm!

In 2000, Wayne sold his original partnership agreement for $500. In 2011, the agreement was sold at auction for $1.6 million!

> *Some people give up too easily!*

In his autobiography *God In My Corner: A Spiritual Memoir*,[1] George Foreman tells the following story:

> Someone once asked an elderly woman her favorite Scripture verse. She replied, "And it came to pass."
>
> "And it came to pass? But that doesn't mean anything."
>
> "Yes it does," she answered. "I know that whenever a trial comes, it doesn't come to stay; it comes—to pass. It's not going to be around forever."

This lady may not be a theologian, but she is on to some Bible truth! In the grand scheme of things, the troubles of life are momentary.

Perseverance is a virtue. So is longsuffering. They may look like vices in this age of instant gratification. But trust me, they are manifestations of the presence of the Holy Spirit.

> *"I'm not gonna give up, shut up, or let up . . .*
> *as a matter of fact, I'm just getting warmed up."*
>
> —Zig Ziglar

Did you know that the manuscript for *Animal Farm*, the classic and international bestseller, was rejected by five different publishers? However, George Orwell, the author, refused to be deterred. He kept plugging on until he found a publisher who was willing to publish his work.

Bjorn Borg, winner of eleven Grand Slam singles tennis titles, once said, "My greatest point is my persistence. I never give up in a match. However down I am, I fight until the last ball. My list of matches shows that I have turned a great many so-called irretrievable defeats into victories."

The first book by Stephen King, the iconic thriller *Carrie*, reportedly received thirty rejections, finally causing Mr. King to give up and trash the manuscript. His wife picked up the book from the trash can and encouraged him to resubmit it *one more time*. *Carrie* was eventually published by Doubleday & Co. in 1973 and has sold millions of copies around the world. It has been made into a movie twice. Today, King has written hundreds of books, has sold over 300 million copies, and is undoubtedly one of the bestselling authors of all time.

Susan Boyle became an overnight superstar in April 2009. According to *The New York Times*:

> Ms. Boyle, 48, was a frumpy unknown before appearing as a contestant on "Britain's Got Talent" in April [2009], stunning the judges and audience with a crystal-clear rendition of the song "I Dreamed a Dream" from the musical "Les Misérables." A You Tube clip of that performance became an instant phenomenon. According to Visible Measures, an American company that computes viewership of Internet videos, it has been watched 310 million times in all of its forms.[2]

Boyle's first album, *I Dreamed a Dream*, which was released on November 23, 2009, became the best-selling album in the world for 2009, selling 9 million copies. In September 2010, Boyle was officially recognized by Guinness World Records as having had the fastest-selling debut album by a female artist in the UK and the most successful first-week sales of a debut album in the UK. She was also awarded the record for being the oldest person to reach number one with a debut album in the UK.[3]

Boyle performed for Pope Benedict XVI on his tour of Britain in 2010. In an interview with Piers Morgan on *Piers Morgan's Life*

Stories, aired by ITV1 in London on Thursday, August 11, 2011, Boyle said she had previously auditioned for various talent shows twelve times, and each time she was rejected and told she was not good enough. However, she said she did not want to give up on her dream of becoming a singer! So she continued to audition until she got her breakthrough.

DON'T YOU DARE GIVE UP

"Life has two rules: #1 Never quit.
#2 Always remember rule # 1."

—Anonymous

Let me ask you a question: How much do you want your breakthrough?

It was Zig Ziglar who said, "Never give up. The moment you are ready to quit is usually the moment right before miracles happen." So don't you dare give up!

Hang in there.

Here are five ways to train yourself to persevere:

1. Have the mentality of a winner.

I know this is easier said than done. But it is possible. You need to develop a winning mentality. Remember that you are born of God and have the divine seed dwelling within you. If God is for you, then it is impossible for you to fail. Just think about this: if God gave Jesus Christ (the very best of the best) to die for you when you were his enemy wallowing in sin, now that you have become his child, his heir, and a joint heir with Jesus Christ, do you think he would withhold any good thing from you? I don't think so!

How much do you want your breakthrough?

Sometimes we give up too easily. You must realize at all times that the battle is not over until God says so.

2. Realize that the darkest hour of the night is just one hour before dawn!

You've got to realize that delay is not denial. If you hang in there long enough, the challenge or difficulty will pass. That's not to bury your head in the sand and pretend the problem isn't there. Far from it! Keep working at the challenge. Keep trying to find a solution.

Your troubles won't kill you!

The Bible puts it this way: "Weeping may stay for the night, but rejoicing comes in the morning."[4]

No matter how long it takes, hang in there. Your troubles won't kill you! Remember, as Dr. Robert H. Schuller once said, tough times never last, but tough people do!

3. Focus on the end result!

If Jesus had wanted to give up on the cross, he had a million and one reasons to do so. He was not immune to the temptation to give up—he even prayed that the cup might pass over him. But crucially, he submitted himself to God's sovereign will and held on. Why? Because he saw the joy and the glory that were ahead of him!

Jesus's focus was not on the pain and suffering but on the outcome. Learn from Jesus. Focus on the goal. Imagine what can happen if you don't give in or give up!

4. Have a list of daily affirmations that you make conscientiously.

Your mind is very powerful. So powerful that the Bible says in Proverbs 23:7 that as you think, so you are! Joyce Meyer says that wherever the mind goes, the man follows! Henry Ford put it brilliantly when he said, "Whether you think you can or think you can't—you are right."

Your mind controls your thoughts, which overflow into your actions.

One way to train your mind and make it go in the direction you want

Tough times never last, but tough people do!

is to have a list of daily affirmations to say that reinforce what the Bible says about you. You can repeat these on a regular basis. For instance, I often say:

- "I can do all things through Jesus Christ who gives me strength."
- "Every day in every way I am getting better and better!"
- "I am born of God, and I am more than a conqueror!"
- "Because God is for me, nobody can be against me."

Make your affirmations all the time. Make them conscientiously, whether you feel like it or not. Let them become part of your system.

How much do you want your breakthrough? Nothing good comes easily. If it appears easy, it's because somebody has done the hard work! My friend, don't you dare give up on your dreams.

5. Stop and think.

Whenever you feel like quitting, take a moment to stop and think. Go for some fresh air. Do something that will clear your head. You can go for a walk or a drive or even a jog. As you do so, take the opportunity to reflect. Think: What will happen to your dream if you quit? Remember all the investments you've already put into it—your time, money . . . everything! Ask yourself: "Is quitting the best option, or is there another way?"

Denied a job by Facebook in 2009, Brian Acton and Jan Koum cofounded WhatsApp the same year. Five years later in 2014, they sold WhatsApp to Facebook for an incredible $16 billion! They didn't give up!

> *When you give in to your challenges, you abort your dream!!*

When you fail to stay the course or give in to your challenges, you abort your dream and give the devil something to rejoice over! You also disappoint the Lord Jesus, who is waiting for you to enforce the victory he won on your behalf at Calvary. If Susan Boyle can dare to dream, so can you!

Chapter 7:

EXPECT THE MIRACULOUS

"Expect great things from God. Attempt great things for God."

—William Carey

"Very truly I tell you, whoever believes in me will do the works I have been doing, and they will do even greater things than these, because I am going to the Father."

—John 14:12, New International Version

•　•　•

You can tell Matt Abrahamson expected great things from God. He was expectant, and so when Jesus's disciples couldn't help him, he went looking for Jesus himself. He was expecting the miraculous, and he wasn't disappointed.

Shortly after Matt received his miracle, the tax authorities demanded tax money from Peter for Jesus and himself. We are told that Peter paid the tax by fishing—but *not by selling the fish.* He paid the tax by getting money from the mouth of the first fish he caught!

Anybody can sell fish to make money. But only those who know their God can cause money to come

Know God. Be strong. Do exploits!

from the mouth of a fish. The Bible says, "The people that know their God shall be strong, and do exploits."[1] Know God. Be strong. Do exploits!

THIS IS YOUR TIME

As we've seen, nothing should be impossible for you. You have the power of life and death in your mouth. You have all the resources of heaven at your disposal. There is no height you cannot scale. There is no river you cannot cross. There is no obstacle you cannot surmount as long as you set your heart to it, because the force that originated the universe is on your side. And you can do all things through Christ who gives you strength.[2]

> *You can do all things through Christ who gives you strength!*

The Bible tells us that the whole of creation is groaning and waiting in eager anticipation for *your* manifestation as a son of God.[3] If there was ever a time for Christians to exercise their right to be children of God, it is now! The world is crying out for people who can do exploits because they know their God.

This is the time to arise and shine and bring glory and honor to God. Mankind is desperately waiting for people who will display the manifold wisdom of God. Even the Lord Jesus Christ is waiting . . . for his enemies to be made his footstool. You make Jesus's enemies into his footstool by enforcing the victory Jesus won on the cross of Calvary over two thousand years ago. You do this as you exercise your authority as a believer and live your life in victory.

BUT FIRST EMBRACE FORGIVENESS

Unforgiveness is a silent killer that blocks the flow of God's blessings. Anne Lamott once said, "Not forgiving is like drinking rat poison and then waiting for the rat to die."

Forgiveness is a double-edged sword. It has two edges and works both ways. You need to forgive others. You must learn to forgive everyone who hurts you, whether they deserve it or not. You must also learn to accept forgiveness, especially when God forgives you!

C.S. Lewis put it brilliantly when he said, "To be a Christian means to forgive the inexcusable, because God has forgiven the inexcusable in you."

MIRACLES STILL HAPPEN

The miraculous happens around us all the time. However, if you're going to see miracles in your life, you need to align your life with what God says is true—and that means there are several changes you need to make in your thinking. Here are some of the important ones:

1. See yourself the way God sees you: blessed.
You've got to make sense of what God has done for you and see yourself the way he sees you: as blessed, victorious, triumphant, more than a conqueror, and highly favored. In the words of Joel Osteen, "How do you tap in to what God has already done? Very simple: just act like you're blessed, talk like you're blessed, walk like you're blessed, think like you're blessed, smile like you're blessed, dress like you're blessed. Put actions behind your faith, and one day you will see it become a reality."[4]

> To see miracles you need to align your life with what God says is true!

2. Attempt great things for God.
You're God's ambassador here in this world—his representative. Your duty is to make him known.

You attempt great things for God:

- As you live in obedience and depend utterly on him.
- As you demonstrate his love in sharing the good news of salvation in Christ.

- As you demonstrate his power in praying for the sick.
- As you demonstrate his compassion in caring for the needy and less fortunate.

3. Align your language with the Word.

Words are extremely powerful. Be very careful of what you say concerning yourself and those under your care.

There is a difference between the facts and the truth. The facts are what you may be experiencing at a particular point in time in your life, while the truth is what God's Word says about the particular situation you currently face—for instance, "Is anything too difficult for the Lord?"[5]

Confess and proclaim the truth of God's Word, not the fact of your daily struggles! Here are some declarations I suggest you make every day:

- I am God's child, for I am born again of the incorruptible seed of the Word of God, which lives and abides forever (1 Peter 1:23).
- I am a new creature in Christ (2 Corinthians 5:17).
- I am the righteousness of God in Christ Jesus (2 Corinthians 5:21).
- I am a spirit being alive to God (Romans 6:11, 1 Thessalonians 5:23).
- I am a believer, and the light of the gospel shines in my mind (2 Corinthians 4:4).
- I am God's workmanship, created in Christ unto good works (Ephesians 2:10).
- I am a doer of the Word and blessed in my actions (James 1:22–25).
- I am a joint heir with Christ (Romans 8:17).
- I am more than a conqueror through Jesus who loves me (Romans 8:37).
- I am an overcomer by the blood of the Lamb and the word of my testimony (Revelation 12:11).
- I am a partaker of God's divine nature (2 Peter 1:3–4).

- I am an ambassador for Christ (2 Corinthians 5:20).
- I am a chosen generation, a royal priesthood, a holy nation, a special person purchased by Christ (1 Peter 2:9).
- I am the temple of the Holy Spirit; I am not my own (1 Corinthians 6:19).
- I am the head and not the tail; I am above only and not beneath (Deuteronomy 28:13).
- I am the light of the world (Matthew 5:14).
- I am God's elect, full of mercy, kindness, humility, and long-suffering (Romans 8:33, Colossians 3:12).
- I am forgiven of all my sins and washed in the blood of Jesus (Ephesians 1:7).
- I am delivered from the power of darkness and translated into God's kingdom (Colossians 1:13).
- I am redeemed from the curse of sin, sickness, and poverty (Deuteronomy 28:15–68, Galatians 3:13).
- I am firmly rooted, built up, established in my faith, and overflowing with gratitude (Colossians 2:7).
- I am called of God to be the voice of God's praise (Psalm 66:8, 2 Timothy 1:9).
- I am healed by the stripes of Jesus (Isaiah 53:5, 1 Peter 2:24).

4. *Expect God to do you good.*

God wants to do you good. He delights in your well-being and prosperity. He wants you to enjoy your everyday life.

Wake up each morning expecting the miraculous. As you go about your day, expect God to do you good. Get up every day with this attitude: "I am a child of God. God's mercies are new every morning. Therefore, I can't wait to see what God will do in my life today!"

Joel Osteen put it this way: "You've got to believe that you've not laughed your best laugh *yet*. You've not sung your best song, *yet*. You've not danced your best dance, *yet*. You've not lived your best life, *yet*. Your best life is still out in front of you. So stay connected to God. Stay in faith."

5. *Give praise for all things.*

Learn to see God's hand as behind every good thing that comes your way. As you go through your day, give praise for every mercy you receive, no matter how small it may seem. Don't take anything for granted.

Thank God for that parking space. Give praise for the traffic lights that turn green at the right time. Thank him for the bus, train, or airplane that is on schedule. Give praise for the bargain at the mall.

Giving thanks for small things helps us see the miraculous where it's really occurring. It puts our daily struggles into perspective. It shows us the truth about the life we're living and keeps us from taking God for granted.

MIRACLES STILL HAPPEN TO EVERYDAY PEOPLE!

God uses his power and love to work for and on behalf of all his creation through his provision, protection, and emotional and physical healing. The greatest miracle of all is still available today— salvation in Christ Jesus.

Change your perspective of the miraculous, and instead of coincidences, see *God-incidences!* You will notice how blessed you are. Some things that happen to you will make you shout, "Wow, that's a miracle!" Others may be more subtle, but if properly identified, they will help you see God at work in transforming you *daily* into the image of Jesus Christ.

> *Change your perspective and instead of coincidences, see God-incidences!*

Epilogue:

THE WORD *IMPOSSIBLE* SHOULDN'T BE PART OF YOUR VOCABULARY!

"We have a crop of young people to whom nothing is impossible."

—Walt Disney

"Jesus replied, 'Truly I tell you, if you have faith and do not doubt, not only can you do what was done to the fig tree, but also you can say to this mountain, "Go, throw yourself into the sea," and it will be done.'"

—Matthew 21:21, New International Version

•   •   •

There's no impossibility with God. With him, all things are possible. I sincerely believe that the word *impossible* has never been a part of God's vocabulary. I base this belief on my life experiences as well as my understanding of Scripture. And if *impossible* isn't part of God's language, it shouldn't be part of yours either!

Jesus said, "Have faith in God . . . Truly I tell you, if anyone says to this mountain, 'Go, throw yourself into the sea,' and does not doubt in their heart but believes that what they say will happen, it will be done for them."[1] Your mountain is, of course, any challenge, problem, or difficulty that you find overwhelming.

THERE'S A DIVINE SOLUTION IN PLACE

When Jesus told his listeners to "have faith in God," he was asking them to recognize that *God had provided a divine solution* even before the mountain came into existence. With this understanding, Jesus expects you to face up to your mountain. Be specific: identify your mountain, if possible,

> *God provided a divine solution even before the mountain came into existence!*

by name. Then speak to the mountain and command it to move. As long as you do not doubt, the mountain will move, and nothing will be too difficult for you.

Dr. Robert H. Schuller describes the effect of the words "impossibility" and "it's possible":

Consider . . . that dirty thirteen-letter word *impossibility*. When uttered aloud, this word is devastating in its effect. Thinking stops. Progress is halted. Doors slam shut. Research comes to a screeching halt. Further experimentation is torpedoed. Projects are abandoned. Dreams are discarded. The brightest and best of the creative brain cells nose-dive, clam up, hide out, cool down and turn off in some dark, subterranean corner of the mind . . .

> *The effects of having the word impossible in your language are terrible!*

But, let someone utter the magic words *It's possible*. Those stirring words, with the siren appeal of a marshalling trumpet, penetrate into the subconscious tributaries of the mind, challenging and calling those proud powers to turn on and turn out new ideas! Buried dreams are resurrected. Sparks of fresh enthusiasm flicker, then burst into new flame. Tabled motions are brought back to the floor. Dusty files are reopened. Lights go on again in the darkened laboratories . . .[2]

The effects of having the word *impossible* in your everyday language are terrible. Everything can be transformed when we change our language and beliefs.

IMPOSSIBLE IS AN EXCUSE

The word *impossible* is simply an excuse—for mediocrity, incompetence, ineffectiveness, clumsiness, and ineptitude. You don't need an excuse, because you're a masterpiece, a unique creation, wonderfully and lovingly put together by God and full of incredible potential.

Please pay careful attention: *impossible* is a figment of the human imagination. Impossible is like a vapor. Impossible is a mist. Impossible is

> *Impossible is a mirage!*

nothing but an illusion. Impossible is a mirage. Impossible is not a fact. Impossible is an *opinion,* a fabrication of the human mind. Impossible is not real.

Impossible is a lie of the devil, concocted and put together from the pit of hell. Impossible does not exist, because if you have faith as small and as infinitesimal as a mustard seed, nothing shall be impossible for you!

ENDNOTES

Preface: The Word *Impossible* Didn't Exist in the Beginning!

1. Mairi Robinson ed., *Chambers 21st Century Dictionary*. Edinburgh, UK: Chambers, 1996. 678
2. Mairi Robinson ed., *Chambers 21st Century Dictionary*. Edinburgh, UK: Chambers, 1996. 1532
3. https://en.oxforddictionaries.com/definition/impossible
4. Mairi Robinson ed., *Chambers 21st Century Dictionary*. Edinburgh, UK: Chambers, 1996. 1083.
5. Strong's Number 101. *New Strong's Concise Dictionary of the Words in the Greek Testament*. Nashville: Thomas Nelson, 1995.
6. Matthew 17:14–27 (MSG)

Chapter 1: Connect with the Divine

1. Colossians 1:16–17 (MSG)
2. Blaise Pascal, quoted in: W. Bright, *Jesus and the Intellectual*, Campus Crusade for Christ International, Arrowhead Springs, San Bernardino, CA, 1968.
3. Wayne Stiles, "Essential Choices Help Destroy the Painful Void in Your Life" http://www.waynestiles.com/2-essential-choices-help-destroy-the-painful-void-in-your-life/
4. John 10:9–10 (MSG)

Chapter 2: Discover Your Purpose

1. Ephesians 1:11 (MSG)
2. Mark 1:16–18
3. Luke 23:26
4. Genesis: 45 3–8
5. Matthew 7:7–8 (NKJV)

Chapter 3: Let Vision Guide You

1. Hebrews 12:2
2. Genesis 37: 9–10
3. John Maxwell, "Destiny Calling? Let VISION Be Your Guide." *JohnMaxwellonLeadership.com.* http://johnmaxwellonleadership.com/2010/02/19/destiny-calling-let-vision-be-your-guide/
4. Habakkuk 2:2 (KJV)
5. "About Walt Disney" *Walt Disney Archives*, https://d23.com/walt-disney-archives/about-walt-disney/

Chapter 4: Maximize Your Potential

1. Please see http://thehumancalculator.com/
2. Mark 9:23 (NLT)
3. 1 Corinthians 4:2
4. Zechariah 4:10
5. Ecclesiastes 9:10 (NLT)
6. 2 Timothy 4:6–7 (NIV)

Chapter 5: Dare to Believe

1. Philippians 4:13 (NLT)
2. Mark 5:34 (GWT)
3. Matthew 17:20 (NIV)
4. Aquanetta Gordon, *Echoes of an Angel: The Miraculous True Story of a Boy Who Lost his Eyes but Could Still See.* Carol Stream, IL: Tyndale, 2014. 64
5. Genesis 27:39-40 (MSG)
6. http://www.forbes.com/profile/amancio-ortega/
7. http://www.bbc.co.uk/news/business-37317369
8. James 2:17
9. Genesis 24:27 (KJV)

Chapter 6: Ride Out the Storm

1. George Foreman, *God In My Corner: A Spiritual Memoir (Hardcover)*. Nashville: Thomas Nelson, 2007. 132

2. Ben Sisario, "Susan Boyle, Top Seller, Shakes Up CD Trends," *The New York Times,* 2 December 2009. http://www.nytimes.com/ 2009/12/03/arts/music/03sales.html

3. "Susan Boyle celebrates after getting THREE Guinness World Records," *Daily Mail* (London), 19 September 2010. http://www.dailymail. co.uk/tvshowbiz/article-1313401/Susan-Boyle-celebrates-getting-THREE-Guinness-World-Records.html

4. Psalm 30:5 (NIV).

Chapter 7: Expect the Miraculous

1. Daniel 11:32 (NIV)

2. Philippians 4:13

3. Romans 8:22

4. Joel Osteen, *I Declare: 31 Promises to Speak Over Your Life.* Philadelphia, PA: Running Press, 2014. 102.

5. Genesis 18:14 (NASB)

Epilogue: The Word *Impossible* Shouldn't Be Part of Your Vocabulary!

1. Mark 11:22–23 (NIV)

2. Dr. Robert H. Schuller, *Tough Times Never Last, But Tough People Do!* New York, NY: Bantam Books, Reissue edition 1984. 141

ABOUT THE AUTHOR

Pedro Okoro is a pastor, author, success coach, and blogger. He lives in Surrey, United Kingdom, with his wife and their two gorgeous daughters.

CONNECT WITH PEDRO ON SOCIAL MEDIA:

On Facebook: https://www.facebook.com/pedrookoro7

On Twitter: https://twitter.com/Pedrookoro

Via his blog: http://www.pedrookoro.com/

RECEIVE REGULAR INSPIRATION
AND EMPOWERMENT

Never miss an update, special offer, or blog post from Pedro. Simply copy the web address below into your browser to receive regular inspiration and empowerment!*

http://eepurl.com/benwYb

* Pedro guarantees he will never share your e-mail address with anyone else.

www.ingramcontent.com/pod-product-compliance
Lightning Source LLC
Chambersburg PA
CBHW031612040426
42452CB00006B/487